34.

THE SECRET WORLD OF

Snakes

THE SECRET WORLD OF

Snakes

Theresa Greenaway

RAINTREE
STECK-VAUGHN
RSVP **PUBLISHERS**

A Harcourt Company

Austin   New York
www.raintreesteckvaughn.com

Published by Raintree Steck-Vaughn Publishers, an imprint of Steck-Vaughn Company

Acknowledgments
Project Editors: Kathryn Walker, Sean Dolan
Illustrated by Jim Channell
Designed by Ian Winton

Planned and produced by Discovery Books

Library of Congress Cataloging-in-Publication Data
Greenaway, Theresa, 1947-
Snakes / Theresa Greenaway.
p. cm. -- (The Secret World of--)
Includes bibliographical references (p.).
ISBN 0-7398-3510-6
1. Snakes--Juvenile literature. [1. Snakes.] I. Title.
QL666.06 G685 2001
597.96--dc21

00-062830

Printed and bound in the United States
1234567890 LB 05 04 03 02 01

Contents

CHAPTER 1 **Life Without Legs** 6

CHAPTER 2 **On the Move** 12

CHAPTER 3 **Snake Senses** 16

CHAPTER 4 **A Bite to Eat** 20

CHAPTER 5 **Potent Venoms** 26

CHAPTER 6 **Reproduction** 32

CHAPTER 7 **Survival Tactics** 36

CHAPTER 8 **Enemies** 40

GLOSSARY 44

FURTHER READING 46

INDEX 47

CHAPTER 1
Life Without Legs

A snake seems to have an unlikely shape for an animal that catches live prey. It has no legs, a narrow head, and a very long cylindrical body tapering into a tail. Its slender teeth cannot cut flesh or chew. But snakes are widespread and successful predators. Their highly acute sense organs help them to trace and track their prey. Backward pointing teeth grip their catch, and the wide-stretching jaws mean the snake can swallow its victim whole. Some snakes can kill their prey by suffocation, and others inject powerful venom with each bite.

 Most snakes are between 1 foot 6 inches and 6 feet (0.5 and 2 m) long.

 Tiny thread snakes and worm snakes are the smallest, some just 4½ inches (114 mm) long.

 The longest snake ever recorded was a reticulated python that reached 32 feet (10 m). The longest anacondas are slightly shorter, at about 30 feet (9 m).

 Although shorter than a reticulated python, anacondas are much heavier. A large anaconda would weigh over 330 pounds (150 kg).

 Slender vine snakes are about 6 feet (2 m) long, but only about as thick as a little finger!

 The smaller kinds of snakes can live for about 12 years, but some of the larger kinds are known to live for 40 years or more.

Eyes
No eyelids, but protected by a transparent scale called a brille.

Fangs
Pointed teeth for catching prey, and in some species for injecting venom.

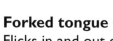

Forked tongue
Flicks in and out constantly, picking up traces of chemicals from the air.

Snakes have been around for at least 90 million years. The earliest fossils found so far date from the Cretaceous Period, when their distant relatives the dinosaurs were alive. Today there are about 2,500 different species, or kinds, of snakes. Most kinds live in the warmer parts of the world, although the European viper, known in Europe as the European adder, can even survive just inside the Arctic Circle.

Skin
Entire outer layer shed when outgrown or old and worn.

Scales
Overlapping scales cover and protect body. Large scales on underside help movement.

Just like other reptiles, this corn snake has a head, neck, body, and tail, but where the neck ends and the tail begins is not easy to see.

SNAKES AND THEIR RELATIVES

Snakes, together with lizards, crocodiles, turtles, and tuatara are all reptiles. Snakes are most closely related to lizards. It is easy to tell a legless snake from a four-legged lizard, although a few lizards such as slow-worms and blind lizards are also legless, or only have tiny hind limbs. Legless lizards can be distinguished from snakes because lizards have ear openings and eyelids, and snakes do not.

All of the snake's internal organs fit neatly one behind the other. The distant ancestors of snakes had two working lungs, but in most modern snakes, only the right one works. The tiny left lung is useless.

Inside the long and narrow body of a snake, organs such as the liver, gut, and kidneys are also long and narrow. Almost all snakes have only one working lung, instead of the usual two. Snakes usually have deeply forked tongues, and, like many other kinds of vertebrate animals, they have a sense organ in the roof of their mouth called the Jacobson's organ.

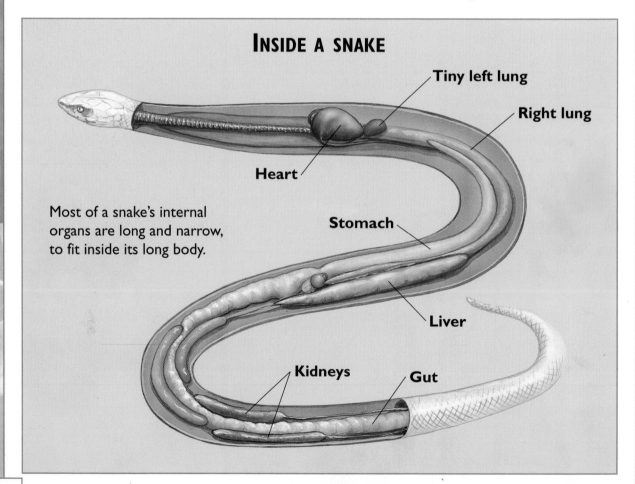

INSIDE A SNAKE

Tiny left lung

Right lung

Heart

Stomach

Most of a snake's internal organs are long and narrow, to fit inside its long body.

Liver

Kidneys

Gut

Snakes and other reptiles are ectotherms, or cold-blooded, which means that they cannot generate very much of their own body heat. Instead they have to live somewhere warm or bask in the sun to bring their temperature up to about 77-86°F (25-30°C). Snakes are most active when they are warm. But they can easily overheat as well and may have to shelter from the midday sun.

Unlike mammals or birds that have an insulating layer of fur or

Garter snakes return to the same site year after year to hibernate when the weather starts to get cold in autumn. Hundreds of garter snakes may hibernate together. They wriggle into cavities under old tree trunks, or under rocks, and do not emerge until it warms up again in the following spring.

feathers, snakes soon lose heat in cool weather. If they are too cold, they cannot move about or digest their food. Snakes that live in places that have cold winters, such as parts of North America or northern Europe, spend the coldest months in hibernation.

SNAKE SKIN

Some people think that snakes are cold and slimy, but this is completely wrong! Snakes are dry and often warm to touch. They are covered with overlapping scales. These scales are part of the outer layers of skin and consist of a protein called keratin, the same substance as your fingernails and hair.

Each kind of snake has scales of a characteristic color or pattern that help to identify it. They may be smooth and glossy, or, like some rattlesnakes, have dull scales. The rough-scaled tree viper has keeled scales that stick out so much that it is sometimes called the hairy or shaggy viper.

The scales covering a snake's belly and sides help it to move along. They also help to protect the snake from damage as it travels over rough surfaces. Because they cover

The gleaming iridescent scales of the Brazilian rainbow boa reflect all the colors of the rainbow as the sunlight shines on them.

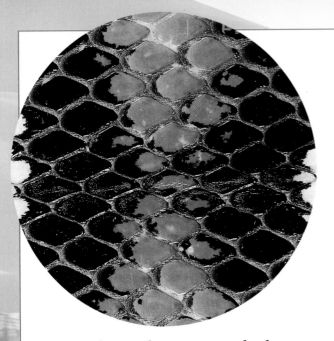

The shiny, smooth scales of a California mountain kingsnake are arranged in distinctive black, red, and white bands.

A BAD REPUTATION

Snakes are feared because it is thought that either they will squeeze people to death or they will kill them with a venomous bite. In fact, many of the most common snakes are neither constrictors nor venomous. They are shy reptiles that are far more likely to slither away and hide than to attack you.

the snake with a watertight layer, scales prevent water from evaporating from the snake's body, so snakes can live in hot, dry places without becoming dehydrated.

The keeled scales of this bush viper are slightly raised so that it looks prickly. This helps this tree-living snake to get a good grip on the bark of twigs and branches.

CHAPTER 2
On the Move

Snakes have a very long, flexible backbone made up of 150 to 430 small bones called vertebrae. There is a pair of ribs for each vertebra, except those of the tail, and a couple right behind the head. People only have about 13 pairs of ribs, but a large snake may have 300 or more pairs!

The backbone and hundreds of ribs support the muscles that make the snake move and also make a cage that protects the internal organs.

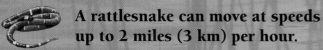

 A rattlesnake can move at speeds up to 2 miles (3 km) per hour.

A racer snake can reach speeds of 4 miles (6.5 km) per hour.

The fastest speed attained by a snake is 7 miles (11.2 km) per hour, by an African black mamba.

The flying tree snake of Southeast Asia spreads its ribs and flattens its body so that it can glide from one tree to another—sometimes an incredible 165 feet (50 m).

Only pythons, boa constrictors and a few other species have the remains of what were once hind legs—two tiny claws on the underside. Without legs, snakes can slither speedily across the ground, swim, bury themselves, climb trees, and a few can even glide through the air. How do they do it?

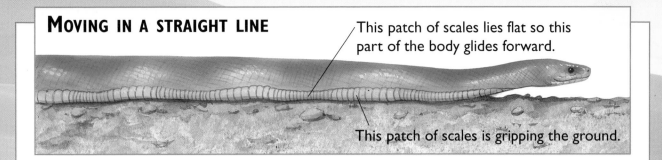

This patch of scales lies flat so this part of the body glides forward.

This patch of scales is gripping the ground.

MOVING ALONG

Along the underside of most kinds of snakes is a single row of large scales. These are attached to muscles. When the muscles relax, these scales lie flat. When the muscles contract, they pull on the base of the scales so that the free edges are raised. The raised scales can grip and dig into the ground. Patches of scales are raised or flattened along the body of the snake so it can glide forward. Smaller scales along the side of the snake are also raised slightly to help the snake as it moves through undergrowth or between rocks.

Large snakes travel over firm ground in a straight line. It looks like magic, but scientists have clearly observed the action of the scales. Traveling through grass or across a forest floor, small and medium-sized snakes wriggle through the undergrowth in

The uneven surface of the ground, together with tufts of grass and other plants, make it easy for a snake to wriggle forward.

When a patch of scales is lying flat, this area stretches forward. Then these scales are raised so that they dig into the ground, and the scales behind flatten and move forward.

serpentine movement. The snake's head weaves from side to side, and the rest of the body follows this path exactly. It feels its surroundings by means of its raised scales and also by pressing the curves of its winding body against the vegetation and bumps in the ground.

SERPENTINE MOVEMENT

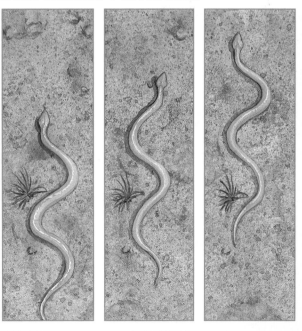

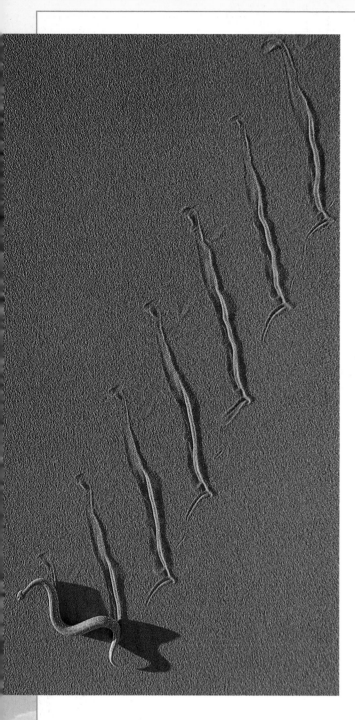

This dwarf sand adder is one of a number of different kinds of snakes that cross the loose, dry sand of desert areas by "sidewinding."

by flinging their head forward to make a curve with the front part of their body. The rest of the body follows successive curves. The overall line of travel is forward, but the head is always facing sideways. Because it looks as though they are moving sideways, these snakes are often known as "sidewinders."

CLIMBING TREES

Tree-climbing snakes use the scales on their underside to get a grip on rough bark or twigs. The coiled or folded lower part of the body grips onto the bark while the head and front part glide up the trunk. Then the snake grips with the front part, and the rear part of its body "acccordions" upwards. To make sure that they do not fall, treesnakes wrap their tails tightly around the branches so they can sleep or strike out at prey in safety.

This Arizona mountain kingsnake shows just how a snake can utilize rough bark to climb a near-vertical tree trunk, even though it has no limbs with which to grasp the trunk.

SIDEWINDERS

The sandy soil of the desert is too loose for a snake's scales to grip. The snakes that live in these deserts travel across the loose sand

Swimming Snakes

Most snakes can swim using a serpentine motion and readily take to water to cross rivers. Grass snakes hunt for frogs and tadpoles in water, and anacondas also lie in wait for their prey in shallow water. Sea snakes, like the one shown below, spend all their lives in water, where they catch and eat fish, squid, and other sea creatures. Some, such as the yellow-bellied sea snake, also give birth in the sea.

Sea snakes are found in the warm coastal seas of tropical Asia, Australia, and parts of the Pacific. Their tails are flattened in the shape of an oar, and act as fins to propel the snake through the water.

CHAPTER 3
Snake Senses

 Racers, whipsnakes, and ribbon snakes hunt by day. They have large eyes with round pupils.

 Nocturnal boas and pythons hunt at night. Their eyes have vertical pupils that look like slits.

 Tree snakes need binocular vision to catch lizards in the treetops. They have eyes with horizontal pupils and narrow snouts so they can see straight ahead and judge distances accurately.

Snakes have to catch food, stay out of danger, and find mates and shelter. But as they have no eardrums and most have poor eyesight, how do they manage to catch sharp-eyed mammals with good hearing that can run fast on four legs? A snake's sense organs help it to do just that. In addition to its senses of sight, hearing, and touch, snakes are able to get a lot of information about the world around them by tasting the air with their tongues. Many can also detect very small changes in temperature.

EYES
Snakes have a staring gaze simply because, without eyelids, they cannot blink. To protect the eyes from scratches, they are covered by a transparent "window" that is part of the skin. Brilles are shed and renewed, together with the rest of the skin, when the snake molts.

Like most snakes that hunt during the day in bright sunlight, the parrot snake has round pupils.

A groove along each side of the narrow snout means that the long-nosed tree snake can see straight ahead and out to each side.

Snakes that hunt for food in daylight have the best eyesight. They are expert at detecting movement but cannot focus on detail or identify stationary objects. At the other extreme, snakes that live underground have very poor vision. The tiny eyes of blind snakes and thread snakes are hidden by scales. They can only tell the difference between light and dark.

The bush viper rests among the leafy branches of a tree during the day. It hunts at night. Like most nocturnal snakes, it has eyes with vertical pupils.

HEARING WITHOUT EARS

Snakes have no external ears or eardrums. Inside their head, there is just one tiny earbone that allows them to hear low-frequency sounds. Instead, with so much of their body in contact with the ground, snakes are very sensitive to vibrations. Because they pick up the vibrations from footsteps or pounding hooves they can glide out of harm's way long before they are spotted by people or trampled by heavy cattle.

▲ This copperhead snake has the deeply forked tongue that is characteristic of almost all snakes.

TASTING THE AIR

A snake has a long, forked tongue that it flicks in and out constantly. It can do this without opening its mouth because the tongue passes through a notch in the upper jaw. As it flicks, the tongue picks up minute traces of airborne chemicals. It also touches the ground, picking up chemicals from there as well.

When the tongue is withdrawn, these chemicals are transferred to openings in the roof of the mouth that lead into a structure called the Jacobson's organ. This identifies the chemicals and sends signals to the brain. Different chemicals have different meanings to the snake. Some may come from a possible mate. Others mean food is close by.

JACOBSON'S ORGAN

This diagram shows where the Jacobson's organ is situated in the roof of the snake's mouth.

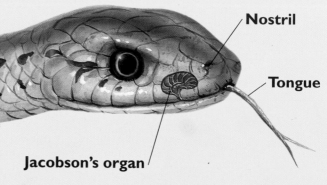

Nostril

Tongue

Jacobson's organ

HEAT DETECTION

Birds and mammals are endotherms, or warm-blooded. This means that they can make their own body heat, so they do not have to bask in the sun to warm up. Many of the snakes, such as rattlesnakes, boas, and pythons, that feed on warm-blooded prey have heat-sensitive pits on their face or mouth.

These pits are so sensitive that the snake can detect changes in temperature of less than 0.002°F (0.001°C). This means that these snakes can not only tell in which direction its prey lies, but also exactly how far away it is. They can strike their prey accurately in complete darkness.

Like rattlesnakes, the eyelash viper has a heat-sensitive pit just in front of each eye. If one pit detects a tiny amount more heat than the other pit, then the snake knows which way to turn toward its prey even though it cannot see it.

CHAPTER 4
A Bite to Eat

All snakes eat flesh or meat of some kind. There are no plant-eating snakes. Some kinds of snakes are not at all fussy about what they eat and will go for anything small enough for it to kill. The garter snake of North America is a good example. It will eat worms, insects, salamanders, tadpoles, frogs, and even small mammals such as voles.

Some snakes eat only warm-blooded mammals. Others prefer insects, fish, frogs, lizards, or even other snakes. A few snakes specialize in eating one kind of

 Snail-eating snakes from South America have long, narrow lower jaws so they can hook their teeth into the flesh of the snail and slowly draw it out of its shell.

 The African snail-eating snake grips the snail's body, then hits it on the ground until the shell breaks.

The thread snake, which is virtually blind, eats ants and termites. It may even live in the termites' nest!

One of the reasons that garter snakes are so widespread and abundant in the United States is because they will eat such a wide range of prey. This snake is swallowing a leopard frog.

Only the largest kinds of snakes, such as this rock python, can overcome and swallow prey as large as a Thomson's gazelle. If it is disturbed while trying to eat it, the snake may regurgitate its meal so it can escape from possible danger.

prey. For example, the annulated sea snake eats only fish eggs. The largest snakes, such as anacondas and pythons, can eat remarkably bulky animals, including goats, caimans, leopards, peccaries, and deer.

A GOOD CATCH

A snake only has its mouth and teeth to catch or pick up prey. Whipsnakes and sandsnakes are examples of active hunters that search for and then chase prey for short distances, but most snakes are content to lie in wait for a suitable dinner to stray too near. From a coiled position, these snakes can lunge their heads forward at lightning speed. This lunge is called a strike.

OVERCOMING PREY

After a successful strike, a snake has to overcome its prey quickly, before it is able to escape or cause injury with its teeth or claws. Anacondas and others of the python and boa family overcome their prey by suffocating it. Gripping the prey with their mouths they wrap their bodies around the victim and constrict its breathing—which is why they are known as "constrictors." Every time the prey breathes out, the snake tightens its grip a little so eventually the victim can no longer breathe in at all and

Once a boa constrictor has thrown its coils around an animal, there is no chance of escape. The snake's powerful muscles contract slowly but steadily, until the trapped victim cannot breathe at all.

dies from suffocation. Large constrictors have been known to kill and eat small adults and children in Africa and Asia.

Venomous snakes all subdue their prey with powerful venom that paralyzes or kills the prey very quickly. Venom is injected by teeth called fangs. Back-fanged snakes, such as mangrove snakes and the boomslang, have grooved fangs towards the back of the jaw. The venom runs down the groove into the wound. These snakes have to work the prey to the back of the mouth in order to deliver their dose of venom.

Front-fanged snakes, such as the taipan and brown snake of Australia, have hollow, venom-injecting fangs in the upper jaw in the front of their mouth. After a strike, they hold onto their prey until the venom takes effect.

Pit vipers such as rattlesnakes, copperheads, and bushmasters, have the most advanced venom-injecting fangs. These long, slender fangs fold back against the roof of the mouth when not in use. When the snake opens its mouth, sets of muscles contract to swing these fangs forward into a stabbing position. Venom is squeezed from large glands by the contraction of other muscles, and it trickles down a canal inside the fang and out through a small opening. A strike from these fangs results in deep stab wounds into the victim's flesh —it takes just a few seconds. Then the snake releases its victim and waits for it to die.

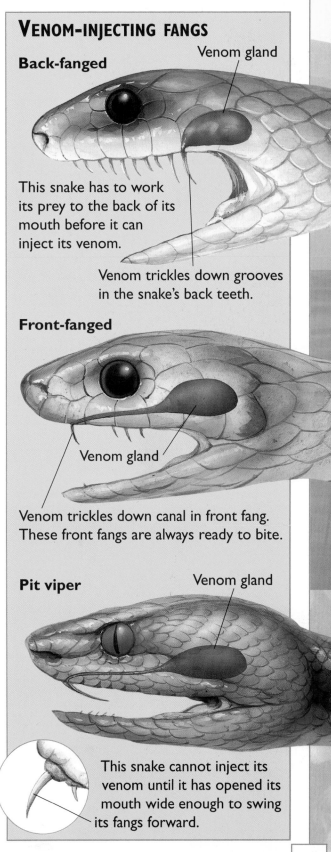

VENOM-INJECTING FANGS

Back-fanged

Venom gland

This snake has to work its prey to the back of its mouth before it can inject its venom.

Venom trickles down grooves in the snake's back teeth.

Front-fanged

Venom gland

Venom trickles down canal in front fang. These front fangs are always ready to bite.

Pit viper

Venom gland

This snake cannot inject its venom until it has opened its mouth wide enough to swing its fangs forward.

SWALLOWED WHOLE

Once subdued, the snake manipulates its prey so it can swallow it head first. This way, limbs are less likely to get caught up in the snake's jaws. Snakes cannot bite off pieces of food, so all prey is swallowed whole.

A snake has to open its mouth really wide to engulf an animal that may be even larger than its own head. So this can happen, the bones that make up the snake's skull are very loosely connected to each other. The lower jaw can completely "unhinge" from the upper jaw. Each half of the lower jaw can move apart. The skin around the jaws is very elastic, so it does not tear. Swallowing the prey takes a long time. The victim is worked back into the throat by alternating movements of each half of the lower jaw, helped by the backward pointing teeth.

A large meal makes quite a bulge in the snake's body as it is squeezed down into its stomach. It also takes

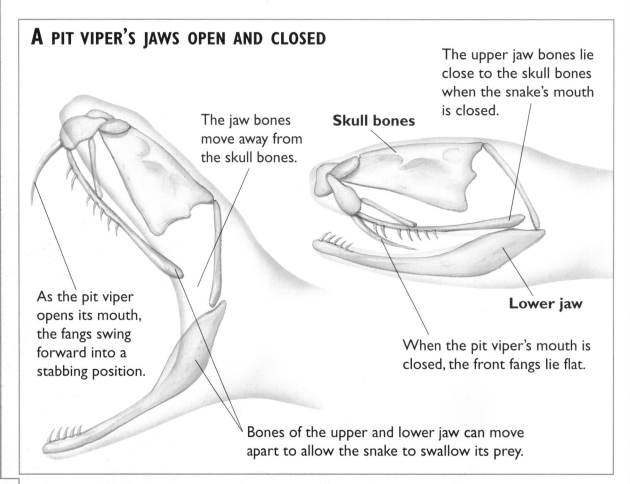

A PIT VIPER'S JAWS OPEN AND CLOSED

The jaw bones move away from the skull bones.

The upper jaw bones lie close to the skull bones when the snake's mouth is closed.

Skull bones

Lower jaw

As the pit viper opens its mouth, the fangs swing forward into a stabbing position.

When the pit viper's mouth is closed, the front fangs lie flat.

Bones of the upper and lower jaw can move apart to allow the snake to swallow its prey.

African egg-eating snakes stretch their mouths open wide to engulf entire eggs. As the egg is squeezed down the snake's throat, the shell is broken by sharp projections from the backbone. Only the nutritious contents pass into its stomach; after a while, a pellet of eggshell is regurgitated by the snake.

I DIDN'T KNOW THAT

▲ As this timber rattlesnake swallows its prey, its throat stretches so much that the skin between the scales can be seen clearly.

a long time to digest, perhaps as long as several weeks if the meal has been a large one. But after a big meal, a snake has no need to eat again for a long time. Anacondas or large pythons may not feed for up to a year after swallowing something the size of a deer or leopard.

CHAPTER 5
Potent Venoms

Snake venom is really a kind of saliva. Some snake venoms are only mildly toxic, but others are lethal mixtures of different chemicals, each of which affects the victim in a different way. The main purpose of these potent venoms is to kill the prey as quickly as possible to prevent it from escaping or hurting the snake. As well as paralyzing or killing the prey, the venom also begins the process of digestion, which is important for an animal that cannot chew its food. Only about 10 percent of snakes have venom strong enough to be dangerous to humans.

► As this copperhead snake starts to open its mouth, its fangs start to swing forward. When the jaw is fully opened, the needle-sharp fangs are poised like daggers to inject a dose of lethal venom.

 Between 30,000 and 40,000 people worldwide die every year as a result of snake bite.

 In the United States, 1,000 bites by venomous snakes occur every year (mostly to people whose jobs involve handling snakes). Of these, only 15 result in death.

 The eastern and western diamondback rattlesnakes are the most dangerous venomous snakes in the United States. Their venom can kill a grown man in one hour.

 The saw-scaled viper is thought to have the most potent venom. It is a small snake that causes many deaths among farmers in Africa, the Middle East, and Central Asia.

 The largest venomous snake is the king cobra from Asia. It is about 16 feet (4.8 m) long when full-grown.

 Vipers inject larger amounts of venom than cobras of the same size, but the venom of cobras is more toxic.

 In 1991, an Australian man bitten on the hand by a brown snake died in 35 minutes.

 The gaboon viper has the longest fangs of all snakes. They are 2 inches (5 cm) long.

HOW VENOMS WORK

The substances contained in snake venoms are divided into groups according to how they affect the victim. One group affects the nervous system, causing heart and respiratory failure. Another group destroys red blood cells. A third group destroys muscles. The fourth group also affects the blood, either by making it clot too freely or by causing severe bleeding. Viper venom generally contains more substances that act on blood.

Cobra venom mostly affects the nervous system of victims.

THE MOST VENOMOUS

A bite from a snake with highly toxic venom can cause an adult human to die in a very short time unless the correct antidote is administered. Snakes with venom

Although gaboon viper venom is not quite as toxic as cobra venom, the amount of venom that the gaboon viper injects with each bite is much larger.

A well-camouflaged rattlesnake is hard to see. Often the first sign of its presence is the warning rattle. Ignoring this can result in a dangerous bite.

that is powerful enough to cause human deaths are found in all three groups of venomous snakes—front-fanged, back-fanged, and pit vipers.

The most venomous snakes in the world are the front-fanged smooth-scaled snake and the eastern brown snake. The snakes that cause most fatalities around the world include the Indian and Egyptian cobras, fer-de-lance, coral snakes, puff adders, and some species of rattlesnakes. People are not the natural prey of snakes. Snakes prefer to avoid conflict and usually flee from people if possible. But they will bite in self-defense especially if they have been accidentally trodden on or disturbed.

Anyone handling a venomous snake is also at risk—even snake experts are bitten from time to time! Female king cobras are one of a few kinds of snake that may be aggressive. They will chase anyone that goes too close to their nest.

A disturbed or threatened cobra rears up and spreads its hood. If its enemy does not retreat, the snake lunges forward and may bite. The cobra family has extremely toxic venom.

ANTIVENINS

If anyone is bitten by a snake suspected of being venomous, it is important to know which kind of snake it was so that the correct antidote can be given. Antidotes to snakebites are produced from the venom itself and are called antivenins. Venomous snakes are kept specially so that supplies of venom can be obtained from them. The snake is "milked" of its venom by pressing its upper jaw against the side of a glass container. This squeezes the venom glands so that the venom trickles down its fangs and into the glass.

▲ This snake is being "milked" of its venom. This does not harm the snake, and the process can be repeated when the snake's venom glands are full again.

The king cobra needs its highly potent venom to overcome the other snakes on which it feeds, but if people disturb it, they too will get a very dangerous bite.

Small but increasing doses of venom are injected into a horse over a period of about three months. The horse builds up immunity against the venom. Amounts of blood are then extracted from the horse, and the serum is separated from it. This serum is then known as an antivenin.

The wounds caused by a snake's fangs are often no more than tiny punctures, but much damage can

be done by the venom, even when antivenins are successfully given. This damage takes a long time to heal. The reason is because the venom destroys muscle, nerve, or blood tissues in a big area around the site of the bite. This often results in large, permanent scars.

CHAPTER 6
Reproduction

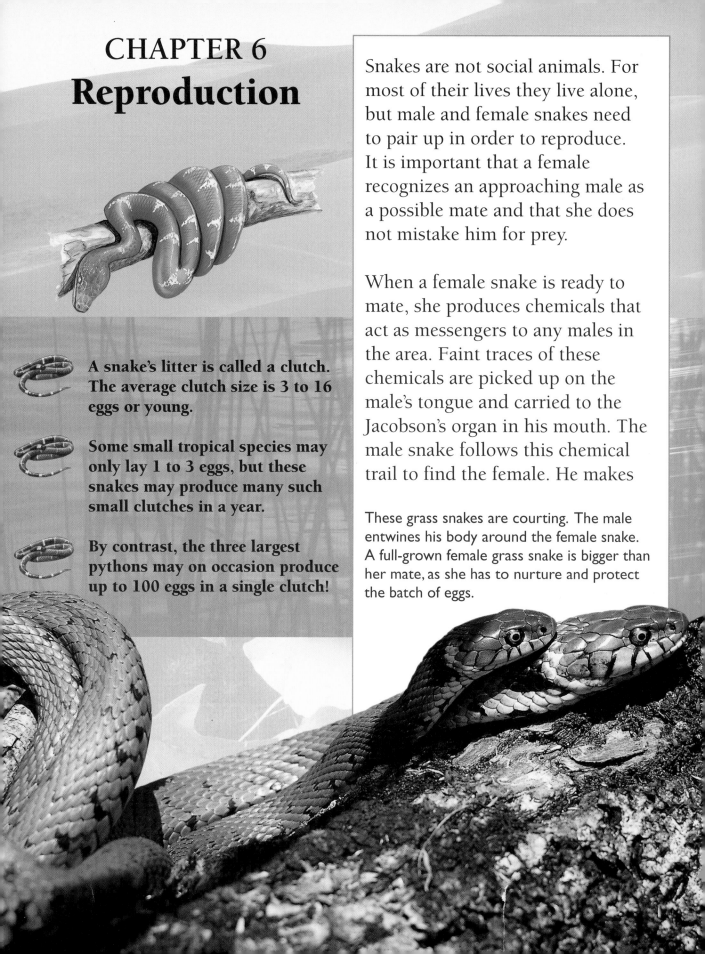

A snake's litter is called a clutch. The average clutch size is 3 to 16 eggs or young.

Some small tropical species may only lay 1 to 3 eggs, but these snakes may produce many such small clutches in a year.

By contrast, the three largest pythons may on occasion produce up to 100 eggs in a single clutch!

Snakes are not social animals. For most of their lives they live alone, but male and female snakes need to pair up in order to reproduce. It is important that a female recognizes an approaching male as a possible mate and that she does not mistake him for prey.

When a female snake is ready to mate, she produces chemicals that act as messengers to any males in the area. Faint traces of these chemicals are picked up on the male's tongue and carried to the Jacobson's organ in his mouth. The male snake follows this chemical trail to find the female. He makes

These grass snakes are courting. The male entwines his body around the female snake. A full-grown female grass snake is bigger than her mate, as she has to nurture and protect the batch of eggs.

contact with the female, eventually twining around her. If there are more males than females, then each female may be surrounded by males, making a ball of intertwined snakes. After mating, males and females go their separate ways.

EGG-LAYING SNAKES

Most kinds of snakes, including thread snakes, pythons, ratsnakes, and kingsnakes, lay oval or elongated eggs with tough, leathery shells. Female egg-laying snakes often choose heaps of rotting vegetation in which to lay their eggs. As this decomposes, heat is generated, which makes a warm, damp environment in which the embryos can develop inside the eggs. A few snakes coil round their eggs.

The Indian python coils around her clutch and twitches, which is thought to help keep the eggs warm.

During incubation, moisture and oxygen are absorbed through the egg shell. The egg swells, sometimes to double its original size. When it is ready to hatch, the tiny snake cuts holes in its shell by using a special egg tooth at the tip of its upper jaw. It may rest in its shell with just its head poking out for a day or so. Then it wriggles free. The hatchling may be as much as seven times longer than its egg!

Hatching is an unhurried activity for a tiny snake. After breaking its shell and poking its head out, the hatchling rests until it feels strong enough to continue.

LIVE YOUNG

In the case of boas and snakes such as cobras, sea snakes, garter snakes, copperheads, and vipers, the eggs stay inside the female until the young are fully developed. The shells of these eggs are no more than thin membranes that split before the eggs are laid, so that the female gives birth to tiny snakes. The embryos of a very few snakes, such as the European viper or adder, are not enclosed in even a thin egg shell. They develop inside the mother and are attached directly to her.

YOUNG SNAKES

Young snakes are independent from hatching or birth. Many look

The dull scales and cloudy eyes of this grass snake indicate that it is about to molt. After molting, the color of the scales is especially bright.

just like miniature versions of their parents, but some have different patterns or colors that help them to hide away while they are still small and vulnerable. The venom of even tiny young venomous snakes is every bit as potent as that of the full-grown snake.

MOLTING

Although a snake's skin can stretch to allow large meals to pass along, snakes, like all reptiles, need to shed their old skin, or molt, as they grow. When a snake is about to molt, it stops feeding and hides away somewhere safe.

The old, discarded skin is crumpled and inside out, but the scales are all clearly visible. A snake does not eat for a few days before molting, so the freshly molted snake may be very hungry.

Molting starts with the secretion of a milky liquid between the old layer of skin and the new layer beneath it. This makes the eyes cloud over. After 2-3 days, the eyes clear. After a few more days, the snake rubs its snout against a rough surface until the old skin splits. It wriggles free, and the skin is shed in one piece. Younger, faster-growing snakes molt more frequently than older snakes.

CHAPTER 7
Survival Tactics

A snake has few of the usual means by which an animal defends itself. It lacks hard hooves or sharp claws, spines, or horns, and is at a clear disadvantage when faced with a hungry, four-legged predator. Because of this, a snake generally prefers to avoid conflict rather than to do battle. If it is cornered by a predator, or has a nest of eggs to

This red diamondback rattler is just one of at least 30 different kinds of rattlesnakes. They are found from Canada in the north to Argentina in South America.

 The rattlesnake is named for the sinister warning rattle at the end of its tail. If this is ignored, the rattler will strike, injecting its dose of potent venom.

 The rattles are made of loose, empty horny segments that rustle against each other when shaken.

A new segment is added every time the rattlesnake molts, but older ones may drop off, so there are never more than 9 or 10 "rattles."

 When in danger, some snakes produce a large amount of very smelly droppings and then roll in them! This makes them less attractive to a predator.

 If they cannot escape or scare away an attacker, all snakes, whether venomous or not, will repeatedly bite anything that threatens them.

Harmless regal ringneck snakes try to stay out of sight, camouflaged by their mud-brown coloring, but if one is exposed or threatened, it either coils its tail to show its bright red underside or flips right over, revealing a startling, bright orange belly.

defend, a snake usually attempts to scare away the enemy by threatening to attack. But if all else fails, then whether venomous or not, snakes bite to protect themselves.

Scaring a predator off can be a good way to avoid ending up as the next meal. A common snake threat is hissing, which will scare many birds and mammals—including people. Boomslangs and hog-nosed snakes can puff up their throats when under threat, and puff adders inflate their whole body to make themselves look bigger.

A few species rely on sudden displays of color, either by opening the jaws wide to reveal the pink mouth, or, as in the case of the ringneck snake, raising and coiling the tail to reveal a red underside. This may not sound scary to you, but many birds are easily frightened by sudden flashes of unexpected color.

CAMOUFLAGE

A snake's scaly skin is often colored or patterned in such a way that it blends in with its background perfectly. Tree snakes are often green, flecked with yellow or brown, just like leaves. Horned desert vipers are the same color as the desert sand. Snakes such as bushmasters and gaboon vipers that live among scrub or on a forest floor are heavily patterned to look just like dead leaves and twigs.

The Saharan desert viper, like other desert snakes, rocks backward and forward to hide itself in the sand.

WARNING STRIPES

Venomous snakes often avoid being attacked by predators because they are brightly colored or patterned, and some harmless species also stay safe by mimicking them. Venomous coral snakes have a warning pattern of bright orange, black, and white stripes.

Kingsnakes, which are found in the same area, look similar to coral snakes, but they are quite harmless. False coral snakes also look rather like coral snakes, but they only have mild venom.

FEIGNING DEATH

Grass snakes and hog-nosed snakes often pretend to be dead when they are threatened, in the hope that the predator, who may prefer more lively prey, will lose interest. The snake adopts an upside–down position and keeps perfectly still, with its mouth lolling open—but this almost perfect trick is spoiled by the snake's habit of flipping itself upside down again if it is turned over!

Spitting Cobras

As well as spreading their necks to make their heads look larger, spitting cobras have venom ducts that open at the front of each fang. They can eject a stream of fine droplets of venom straight into an attacker's eyes up to a distance of about 10 feet (3 m), causing blindness.

CHAPTER 8
Enemies

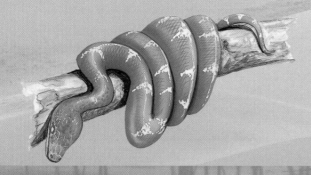

 In the United States, large numbers of harmless snakes are killed because people mistake them for venomous copperhead snakes.

 The timber rattlesnake is now extinct in many parts of its natural range because people have killed and eliminated them from places near human settlements.

 There are about 19 species of snakes worldwide that are considered threatened.

 The endangered New Mexico ridge–nose rattlesnake only lives in southern New Mexico. It is at risk from habitat destruction and is now protected.

 Round Island boas occur nowhere else in the world except on this tiny island in the Indian Ocean. They are seriously endangered.

Snakes have many enemies. Predators of many kinds feed on snakes, especially young snakes and smaller species. These predators include birds of prey, hedgehogs, wild dogs, cats, badgers, and racoons. There are also animals that specialize in eating snakes, such as snake eagles. Those that habitually feed on venomous snakes may have some degree of immunity to the venom, or may rely on clever tactics to avoid being bitten. All snakes are most vulnerable when they are young, but even when full-grown, many are still at risk.

Today, however, the most serious enemies of many kinds of snakes, big and small, are people. Although most snakes are completely harmless to us, many people fear these almost as much as the venomous kinds or large constrictors. This fear leads to the killing of snakes that actually benefit people by consuming rats and mice. At the same time, some people try to get the better of snakes. Rattlesnake round-ups in the United States result in many being hunted, killed, and displayed for sport. This is having a serious effect on rattlesnake populations.

Snake skin is made into boots, bags, belts, and trimmings for garments, even though some kinds of snake skin is illegal.

We are also destroying the habitats of snakes by felling tropical forests and draining wetlands. We are building towns and cities where snakes as well as other wildlife once flourished. Many large snakes are still killed for their skin, which is made into fashion accessories, tourist trophies, or used in local medicines.

MONGOOSES

Mongooses eat a variety of insects, small mammals, and birds' eggs but are most famous for their ability to kill and eat venomous snakes. These alert mammals are very quick on their feet and get tired far less quickly than a snake. They dodge the snake's repeated strikes, then kill it by biting the neck just behind the snake's head. A mongoose can successfully overcome a cobra over twice its length. Mongooses seem to be less affected by cobra venom than other mammals.

This mongoose has successfully caught and killed a large snake. It can now take its time and eat its fill.

SNAKE EAT SNAKE

A snake is a perfect shape for another snake to eat. Californian kingsnakes are constrictors with a varied diet that often includes other snakes, even highly venomous rattlesnakes. The king cobra is the world's largest venomous snake, and feeds almost entirely on other snakes. It is an active hunter and will even climb into bushes or up trees when it is chasing its prey.

SNAKE-EATING BIRDS

Many birds of prey catch and eat snakes. The secretary bird is a large bird of prey that lives in the African savannah. It feeds on

This snake has almost swallowed another snake that must have been as large as itself!

snakes, lizards, and rodents. It kills its prey by stamping on it. A venomous snake's attempts to bite the long, hard, scaly legs of the bird are futile. In the United States, roadrunners kill small snakes with a blow to the head before eating them. These fast-moving birds avoid dangerous bites from venomous snakes by speed and agility.

In Asia, serpent eagles eat other small reptiles, frogs, and rodents as well as snakes, but the short-toed eagle of Europe and the brown snake eagle of Africa feed almost entirely on snakes. These eagles kill their prey by crushing it with immensely powerful talons. The brown eagle can even overcome the dangerously venomous boomslang, puff-adder, and black mamba.

Even sea snakes are not always safe from birds of prey. The yellow-lipped sea snakes of Southeast Asian seas come ashore in large numbers to lay their eggs under the rocks. As the young hatchlings wriggle down to the water, they are an easy target for many birds, including the white-bellied sea eagle.

Snakes as Pets

Having a snake for a pet is appealing but is not always a good idea. Snakes often have very exacting requirements and may need living prey. Otherwise they may become sick and die. Some of the snakes that are easier to keep, such as the reticulated python, present another problem. Although only a few inches long when young, this cute pet might one day measure nearly 33 feet (10 m)!

Glossary

ANTIDOTE – A substance that counteracts the effects of venom or poison

ANTIVENIN – A substance prepared from the blood of an animal that has been dosed with small amounts of venom. It contains specific antidotes to that venom

BRILLE – The transparent covering that protects a snake's eyes

CAMOUFLAGE – Colors or patterns that allow an animal to blend in with its background

CONSTRICTOR – A kind of snake that kills its prey by squeezing its body so it cannot breathe

CRETACEOUS PERIOD – The interval in the Earth's history that started about 141 million years ago and finished 65 million years ago

ECTOTHERMS – Animals such as snakes, lizards, and frogs that cannot produce all their body heat

FANGS – Long, slender, pointed teeth

GLAND – An organ in an animal's body that produces specific substances, such as smells or oils

HIBERNATION – The state of very deep sleep in which some animals pass the cold months of winter

JACOBSON'S ORGAN – A structure in the roof of the mouth of snakes and some other kinds of animals that picks up particular kinds of smells

KEEL – A ridge that sticks up from its surroundings; a snake's scale that has a little ridge on it is "keeled"

KERATIN – The protein from which hair, claws, reptile scales, and fingernails are made

MOLTING – Shedding the entire outer layer of skin

PREDATOR – An animal that catches and eats other animals

PREY – An animal that is caught and eaten by another animal

REGURGITATE – To vomit or expel food out of the mouth that has already been swallowed

SENSE ORGANS – Structures such as eyes and ears that detect what is happening in the world and send the information to an animal's brain

SERUM – A straw-colored liquid obtained from blood

SIDEWINDING – The way in which snakes move over loose desert sand

STRIKE – The fast forward movement a snake makes with its head and upper part of its body in order to bite or catch its prey

VENOM – A toxic liquid injected into the body of another animal by means of fangs, claws, or stings

VERTEBRATES – Animals that have backbones, such as snakes, dogs, and people

Further Reading

Bell, Simon. *Eye to Eye: Snakes and Lizards*. New York: Penguin Putnam, 1997.

Coborn, John. *Snakes*. Broomall, PA: Chelsea House, 1999.

Grace, Eric S. *Snakes*. San Francisco: Sierra Club Childrens, 1994.

Maestro, Betty. *Take a Look at Snakes*. New York: Scholastic, 1997.

Mattison, Christopher. *The Snake Book*. New York: DK, 1997.

Acknowledgments
Front cover: Daniel Heuclin/Natural History Photographic Agency; p.9: Ted Levin/Oxford Scientific Films; p.10: Haroldo Palo Jr./Natural History Photographic Agency; p.11 top & bottom: Daniel Heuclin/Natural History Photographic Agency; p.12: Image Quest 3-D/Natural History Photographic Agency; p.14: Carol Hughes/Bruce Coleman Collection; p.15 left: Michael Fogden/Oxford Scientific Films; p.15 right: David B.Fleetham/Oxford Scientific Films; p.16: John Cancalosi/Bruce Coleman Collection; p.17 top: Daniel Heuclin/Natural History Photographic Agency; p.17 bottom: Karl Switak/Natural History Photographic Agency; p.18: Bruce Coleman Collection; p.19: Bruce Coleman Collection; p.20: John Mitchell/Oxford Scientific Films; p.21: Gunter Ziesler/Bruce Coleman Collection; p.22: Joe McDonald/Bruce Coleman Collection; p.25 top: Zig Leszczynski/Animals Animals/Oxford Scientific Films; p.25 bottom: John Visser/Bruce Coleman Collection; p.27: Bruce Coleman Collection; p.28: Bruce Coleman Collection; p.30 top: Hellio & Van Ingen/Natural History Photographic Agency; p.30 bottom: E. Hanumantha Rao/Natural History Photographic Agency; p.31: George McCarthy/Bruce Coleman Collection; p.32: Hellio & Van Ingen/Natural History Photographic Agency; p.33: Zig Leszczynski/Animals Animals/Oxford Scientific Films; p.34: Jane Burton/Bruce Coleman Collection; p.35: Avril Ramage/Oxford Scientific Films; p.36: Zig Leszczynski/Animals Animals/Oxford Scientific Films; p.37: Michael Fogden/Bruce Coleman Collection; p.38: Eyal Bartov/Oxford Scientific Films; p.39: Anthony Bannister/Natural History Photographic Agency; p.41 top: M.Wendler/Okapia/Oxford Scientific Films; p.41 bottom: Michael Freeman/Bruce Coleman Collection; p.42: Michael Fogden/Oxford Scientific Films; p.43: Daniel Heuclin/ Natural History Photographic Agency.

Index

Numbers in *italic* indicate pictures

adder,
    dwarf sand *14*
    European adder or viper 7, *31*, 34
    puff 29, 37
anaconda 6, 21, 22, 25
antidotes 30
antivenins 30, 31

boa 16, 19, 22, *22*, 34
    Brazilian rainbow *10*
    Round Island 40
body temperature 9
boomslang 23, 37
brille 16
brown snake 23, 26,
    Eastern 29
bushmaster 23

camouflage 38, *38*
claws, vestigial 12,
cobra *29*, 34
    Egyptian 29
    king 26, *30*, 42
    spitting 39, *39*
color and pattern 10, *10*, *11*
    displays of color 37, *37*
    warning patterns 38
    of young 35

constrictors 22
copperhead snake *18*, 23, 27, 34
coral snake 29, 38, 39
courting 32, *32*

defense 29, 36-39, *37*, *38*, *39*

ectotherms 9

egg-eating snake 25, *25*
egg tooth 33
eggs 32, 33, *33*, 34
endangered species 40
endotherms 19
eyes 16, *16*, 17, *17*

false coral snake 39
fangs 22, 23, *23*, 27, 30
feeding 6, 20-25, *20*, *25*, 26, 42, *42*
fer-de-lance 29
front-fanged smooth-scaled snake 29

garter snake 9, 20, *20*, 34
grass snake *32*, *34*, 39

hatching 33, *33*
heat detection 19
heat-sensitive pits 19, *19*
hibernation 9, *9*
hissing 37
hog-nosed snake 37, 39

internal organs 8, *8*

Jacobson's organ 8, 18, *18*, 32
jaws 6, 20, 24, *24*

keratin 10
kingsnake 39
    Arizona mountain *14-15*
    California mountain *11*

life expectancy 6
live young 34

mamba, black 12
mangrove snake 22
mating 32, 33

"milking" 30, *30*
mimicry 38
molting 16, 34, *34* , 35, *35*
mongooses 41, *41*
movement 12-15, *13*, *14*, 15

parrot snake *16*
predators 40-43, *41*, *42*
prey 6, 20-23, *20*, *21*, 22, 25, 26, 42, *42*
python 16, 19, 21, *21*, 22, 33
    Indian 33
    reticulated 6, 43, *43*
    rock *21*

racer 12, 16
rattles 36, *36*
rattlesnake 12, 19, 23, 29, *29*, 36, *36*, 40
    Eastern diamondback 26
    New Mexico ridge-nose 40
    red diamondback *36*
    Timber *25*, 40
    western diamondback 26
rattlesnake round-ups 40
regurgitation 21, 25
reptiles 8, 9
reproduction 32-35
ribbon snake 16
ringneck snake 37
    regal ringneck *37*

sandsnake 21
scales 10, 11, *10*, *11*, 13, *13*, 14, *25*
sea snakes 15, *15*, 34, 43
senses and sense organs 6, 8, 16-19, *16*, *17*, *18*, *19*, 32
serum 31
sidewinding 14, *14*
size 6
skeleton 12, *12*, 24, *24*
skin 10, *10*, 11, *11*, 16, 24, 35, *35*, 41, *41*
snail-eating snake 20

snake-eating birds 42
snake-eating snakes 42, *42*
snakebites 22, 23, 26, 28-31
snakes as pets 43, *43*
speed 12
striking 21
swallowing *21*, 24, 25, *25*
swimming snakes 15, *15*

taipan 23
teeth 6, *6*, 20, 21, 24
thread snake 6, 20
tongue 6, 8, 16, 18, *18*, 32
tree-climbing snakes 14, *14-15*
tree snake 14, 16
    flying 12
    long-nosed *17*

venom and venom glands 6, 22, 23, *23*, 26-31, 35, 39
vine snake 6
viper 26, 28, 34
    bush *11*,*17*
    European viper or adder 7, *31*, 34
    eyelash *19*
    gaboon 26, *28*
    Saharan desert *38*
    saw-scaled 26

weight 6
whipsnake 16, 21
worm snake 6

young snakes 34, 35